W9-BMU-844

Your Power Is On!

Joanne,

Psalm
1:3

Blessings!
Sally-a Robert

Purple flower in Halifax, Canada

Your Power Is On!

A Little Book of Hope

Written by *Sally-Ann Roberts* • Photography by *Eric Paulsen* • Foreword by *Robin Roberts*

PELICAN PUBLISHING COMPANY

Gretna 2013

Copyright © 2013
By Sally-Ann Roberts

Photographs copyright © 2013
By Eric Paulsen
All rights reserved

*The word "Pelican" and the depiction of a pelican are
trademarks of Pelican Publishing Company, Inc., and are
registered in the U.S. Patent and Trademark Office.*

Library of Congress Cataloging-in-Publication Data

Roberts, Sally-Ann.
  Your power is on! : a little book of hope / by Sally-Ann Roberts ; photography by Eric
Paulsen ; foreword by Robin Roberts.
       pages cm
  ISBN 978-1-4556-1902-3 (pbk. : alk. paper) — ISBN 978-1-4556-1903-0 (e-book) 1.
Devotional literature. 2. Bible—Quotations. I. Title.
  BV4832.3.R63 2013
  242—dc23
                                                                          2013029661

Scripture taken from the NEW AMERICAN STANDARD BIBLE®, Copyright © 1960, 1962,
1963, 1968, 1971, 1972, 1973, 1975, 1977, 1995 by The Lockman Foundation. Used by
permission.

Printed in the United States of America

Published by Pelican Publishing Company, Inc.
1000 Burmaster Street, Gretna, Louisiana 70053

Contents

White flower in Halifax, Canada

Foreword

My beautiful sister, Sally-Ann Roberts. The irrepressible Eric Paulsen. Once again, these two New Orleans icons complement each other perfectly, just like your morning coffee and beignets.

Eric's breathtaking photographs, Sally-Ann's simple yet powerful words and passages—*Your Power Is On!* would have been a welcome read during my recent health recovery.

Eric's pictures transport you. My longtime friend is a man of many talents and wonderful surprises. Sally-Ann's sweet messages of hope, love, and faith that correspond with the photos leave me feeling at peace, full of serenity.

My beloved sister has frequently shared with me her favorite scripture, usually in a text message or voicemail very early in the morning after a moment of quiet. She often ends by saying, "Your power is on!" I'm blessed to be her baby sista.

I'm thrilled that, with Eric, Sally-Ann is now sharing with others something so authentic and personal. I hope it brings you as much comfort as it has for me.

Blessings to all,

Robin Roberts
Light, Love, Power, Presence

Edwardsville, Illinois

Preface

Franklin Delano Roosevelt said, "When you get to the end of your rope, tie a knot and hang on." Faith is the knot that has allowed my family and my community to hang on through some extraordinary challenges.

Faith is what allowed Lillian Brown to survive sitting on a sweltering rooftop for nineteen hours in the wake of Hurricane Katrina. It was the same faith that allowed her to return and struggle to rebuild her flood damaged home. I will never forget the peace this Katrina survivor exhibited in an interview I had with her months after the storm, when she was seventy-one years old. Lillian Brown said, "Survival is a wonderful thing with the help of God, because we never know what we can do until we are pushed to the edge."

Again and again, I have been pushed to the edge. In the spring of 2002, I had just released my first novel, *Angelvision*. The idea had come to me in a dream about a young man who was angry with God after his younger brother was killed in an accident. For years, I worked on this novel, studying Bible scriptures dealing with death and Heaven. Pelican Publishing Company published the book. On the day of my first book signing, my husband, Willie, complained of a stomach ache. That was Saturday. The following Monday, my husband was in the hospital.

Willie was diagnosed with stage four colon cancer that had metastasized into the liver. Willie Craft, my husband, mentor, and best friend, died the day before Thanksgiving of that same year. One of my mother's favorite hymns that she often played on the piano and sang in our living room was "He knows just how much we can bear." I believe God gave me *Angelvision* as a way to strengthen me for what lay ahead and to bore into my mind and spirit that this life is not all there is.

Willie worried as he neared death about leaving our beautiful children. Judith was a freshman in college, Kelly, a freshman in high school, and our youngest child, Jeremiah, was only in second grade. But I believe all of Willie's worries disappeared after he left this life. Shortly after his funeral, Willie appeared to me in a dream. Beaming with joy, my husband said, "If I knew then what I know now, I never would have worried about anything." You might say that it was just a dream. I don't think so. I believe it was a confirmation of what I had learned writing *Angelvision*. The best is yet to come!

The Lord is my Shepherd; I shall not want. The Shepherd guided my children and me through the loss of Willie, the death of my beloved father, Lawrence Roberts, two years later, and the destruction of our home and community in the tragedy of Hurricane Katrina one year after that. Our Shepherd brought us through my baby sister, Robin's, medical challenges. Robin was diagnosed with breast cancer in 2007. By the grace of God, Robin beat it. But, five years later, she received the earth-shaking news that the radiation and chemotherapy that had cured her of cancer had caused another disease that we had never heard of. Robin had myelodysplastic syndrome (MDS), a blood-production disorder that can lead to leukemia. Robin needed a bone marrow transplant.

Fortunately, I was the perfect genetic match for Robin. In August 2012, while Hurricane Isaac was bearing down on my hometown, I was at Memorial Sloan-Kettering Cancer Center in New York City. The nurses successfully harvested my stem cells for Robin.

The next day, tragedy struck our family again. Mama died.

We made it home in time to see our mother one last time. Mama never took her eyes off of Robin. She couldn't speak, but her eyes communicated to Robin that everything would be okay. God blessed Mama to stay here until she was satisfied that her baby daughter, Robin, had what she needed. The next week, Robin went into the hospital to prepare for the transplant to, by God's grace, receive a new lease on life.

And yes, He knows just how much we can bear. I had someone to hold my hand through Robin's illnesses and mourning Mama's death. My son, Jeremiah, would have a dad to steer him through adolescence into manhood. Ron Nabonne, a family friend, boarded up the doors of my flood-damaged house after Katrina and ultimately opened my heart. I was blessed to marry this prince of a man in 2007.

So now I ask you, what do *you* do when life has disappointed you or when things have not worked out as you planned? I don't know why you picked up this little book of hope. I do know one thing for sure: you are facing something. My sister Robin says that she can't complain about her health challenges because everyone is dealing with something.

Regardless of your wealth, race, residence, or religion, you are going through *something,* and if it is important to you, then it matters. Working in television news for more than three decades, I've experienced thousands of live broadcasts. In fact, all of us are in the middle of a live shot. Life is live! There are no tape delays or instant replays. You've got to live and give it all you've got. You've got to care and bear a whole heck of a lot, because life is live!

What do you do when pushed to the edge? You trust God to give you wings. How do you trust God? By remembering who He is. My sister Dorothy and I flew numerous times from New Orleans to New York this past year to be with Robin, and never once did we cringe in fear during the loud roar of the plane at takeoff or pace the aisles worrying that the heavy aircraft wouldn't carry us to our destination. We had confidence in the pilot. Why not trust the ultimate Pilot in guiding you to your destination, too?

This type of faith doesn't come naturally. It takes time and encouragement. When I was just starting out as a reporter in New Orleans, I was always second-guessing myself and had very little confidence. Each morning before leaving for work, Willie would look me in the eyes and say, "The Power is *on!*" This was his way of calming my insecurities and reminding me to trust God.

It took me years to truly comprehend the enormity of this Power, but I had an awakening. The Buddhist proverb rang true: When the student is ready, the teacher will appear. For me, the Teacher appeared in January 1991 in my darkened bedroom. I was in my thirties and the early morning newscast that I anchored had just been canceled because of a downturn in the economy. I thought I was going to lose my job at WWL-TV. I was alone and desperately needed someone to talk to—but who? Then, as my parents had taught me by their example, I decided to pray. But that didn't ease my anxiety, so I pulled out a notebook and I wrote a letter to God.

I carefully wrote down my laundry list of concerns and ended the tear-stained letter with "Amen." Out of the blue, an unusual thought came to mind: "Now listen." That day, I sat quietly, and something wonderful happened. Comforting thoughts began to fill my mind. They were so encouraging that a refreshing peace washed over me. I began writing down the thoughts as quickly as they occurred to me. That day, I started the first of what would become countless Prayer and Listening Journals.

That day in January 1991 transformed my relationship with prayer. I see prayer now as two-way communication. God's voice is not like a human voice. The Holy Spirit speaks to the heart. It's hard to explain—I just feel His direction and His love. Now, I enjoy taking time to pray, read the Bible, and then sit quietly. I write down my prayers and I write down what I receive from the Holy Spirit. From time to time, I reread old journals. They are a constant reminder of the goodness of God and all that he has brought my family through.

This is how I connect with my Creator. This is what works for me. I'm not saying that it works for everyone—everyone's relationship with the Lord is personal and individual.

What really inspired me to write this little book of hope was my sister Robin's illness. It was the proverbial straw that broke the camel's back. Even though I had been through so much heartache, the thought of losing my baby sister was too much. My family and I had to press into our faith. Now, I feel the need to share what I have learned on this walk of faith. As Mama always said, "Make your mess your message."

My spirit received this message. It is for me, and I hope for you, a glorious reminder of the majesty and grace of our Creator. All through my highs and lows, I leaned heavily on this message and some of the encouraging Bible verses you will find on the pages of this book. God has a plan for your life and mine. He will guide us if we take the time to listen.

The Lord speaks to us through His creation. It is captured in the beautiful photography of my good friend and WWL-TV colleague Eric Paulsen, who has been with me through all of the ups and downs. Wherever you are on this journey of life, I hope that, as you gaze at Eric's photographs, you feel God's love for you.

Remember, God loves *you*.

Whatever you are facing today or will face in the future, be encouraged: your Power is *on!*

Lawrence and Lucimarian Roberts

Left to right: *Robin, Dorothy, Sally-Ann, and Lawrence*

Author's Note

This book is dedicated to my parents, Lawrence and Lucimarian Roberts.

Now that we must carry on without them, I see so many of the qualities of my parents in my wonderful siblings. Lawrence Roberts II exhibits their wisdom and resolve. Dorothy Roberts McEwen has inherited their strength and spirituality. Robin Roberts lives her life with the courage and compassion that our parents modeled for us every day of their lives.

Thank God for family.

Photographer's Note

When Sally-Ann first approached me about combining her words with my pictures, while flattered, I wasn't sure how they might correspond. Then, I began reading what she wrote and looking over some of my photographs.

I love shots of nature. From a sunset to the majesty of a mountain in Oregon to the tiniest detail of a flower, it is not hard to see the hand of God at work. Hopefully, you enjoy these pictures and Sally-Ann's words. I believe they do complement each other and illustrate her inspiring message.

I dedicate this work to my wife and best friend, Bethany.

Sunset in Italy

Acknowledgments

It is easier to start a project than to it is to finish. I would like to thank all of my family and friends who encouraged me to get to the finish line. I thank God for my loving children: Jeremiah Craft; Kelly and her husband, Jeremy Tatum; and Judith Craft and my soon-to-be son-in-law Tony Champagne Jr. I also thank God daily for my grandson, Elijah Tatum, who knew how to pray from the heart by the age of five. It's something that was honed into him by his prayer-warrior grandmother Carol Tatum and great-grandmothers Ella Mae Craft, Gloria Bush, and Lucimarian Roberts.

Thank you, Lord, for my daily prayer partners: my wonderful sister-in-law Phyllis Alexander and dear friends Cathy Harris and Pattie Shoener. I thank God for all of my prayer-warrior friends and family, including but not limited to Lisa Martin, Al Mims, and my sister-in-law Claudette Griggs, who has a knack for sending inspirational text messages when I need them most. My father-in-law, Pierre André Nabonne, a World War II veteran and Bronze Star recipient, continues to bless me with his wit and wisdom.

Thank you, Lord, for Earth angels Susan and Tracy Krohn, who opened up their beautiful home to me for the year and a half it took to rebuild my house after Hurricane Katrina. Thank you, Lord, for Earth angel neighbors Willie Jordan and his wife, Geraldine, who helped me rebuild my house as they were rebuilding their own.

Thank you, Lord, for Angela Hill, Craig Schwartzenberg, Dr. Brobson Lutz, Anjelé Simien, Larry Everage Jr., Ray Harris, Val Amedee, Dr. Kevin Stephens, and Dominic Massa, who offered encouragement and counsel at critical points along my journey.

A heartfelt thanks to Pelican Publishing Company and Eric Paulsen for joining me in this venture.

I am eternally grateful to my husband, Ron Nabonne, for joining me in life's adventure. Thank you, Lord, for this gift.

Finally, I thank God for the doctors, nurses, and technicians who worked tirelessly to save the life of my baby sister, Robin.

Water lilies in Uptown New Orleans, Louisiana

Your Power Is On!

Be still and know that I am God.
I am, I am.

In the beginning God created the heaven and the earth. And the earth was without form, and void; and darkness was upon the face of the deep.

And the Spirit of God moved upon the face of the waters. And God said, Let there be light: and there was light.

Genesis 1:1-3 (KJV)

Bird soaring over Poplarville, Mississippi

I created this world and everything in it. I gave life to you and to every other living thing, plant and animal.

The grass withers, the flower fades,
But the word of our God stands forever.

Isaiah 40:8 (NASB)

Field of daisies in Nova Scotia, Canada

Do you really think that I cannot help you overcome any obstacle?

Deep calls to deep at the sound of Your waterfalls;
All Your breakers and Your waves have rolled over me.
The Lord will command His lovingkindness in the
 daytime;
And His song will be with me in the night,
A prayer to the God of my life.

Psalm 42:7-8 (NASB)

Waterfall near Portland, Oregon

I am, I am.

The Lord *is* my light and my salvation; whom shall I fear? The Lord *is* the strength of my life, of whom shall I be afraid?

Psalm 27:1 (KJV)

Waterfall outside of Portland, Oregon

Waterfall outside of Portland, Oregon

I own the cattle on a thousand hills, and my storehouses are filled to overflowing.

O the depth of the riches both of the wisdom and knowledge of God! how unsearchable *are* his judgments, and his ways past finding out!

Romans 11:33 (KJV)

I am, I am.

Don't you be afraid, for I am with you.
Don't be dismayed, for I am your God.
I will strengthen you.
Yes, I will help you.
Yes, I will uphold you with the right hand of my
righteousness.

Isaiah 41:10 (WEB)

Swamp in Breaux Bridge, Louisiana

What are you afraid of?
If you are afraid of anything but Me,
your fear is misplaced.
Fear Me alone.
I am, I am.

Be not overcome of evil, but overcome evil with good.

Romans 12:21 (KJV)

Landscape of Italy

I give life.

I will give thanks to you,
for I am fearfully and wonderfully made.
Your works are wonderful.
My soul knows that very well.

Psalm 139:14 (WEB)

Family of giraffes at Global Wildlife Center in Folsom, Louisiana

I give peace.

Peace I leave with you. My peace I give to you; not as the world gives, give I to you. Don't let your heart be troubled, neither let it be fearful.

John 14:27 (WEB)

Caribbean Sea

I give joy.

But the fruit of the Spirit is love, joy, peace, patience, kindness, goodness, faith, gentleness, and self-control. Against such things there is no law.

Galatians 5:22-23 (WEB)

Bird in flight over Cozumel, Mexico

Don't fall for the devil's lies.
He would like you to believe that all is lost.
He wants you to give up, cave in, and pack up.

We are pressed on every side, yet not crushed;
perplexed, yet not to despair; pursued, yet not forsaken;
struck down, yet not destroyed . . .

2 Corinthians 4:8-9 (WEB)

Clouds over Uptown New Orleans, Louisiana

*Tell the devil no and keep putting one foot
in front of the other.*

For we walk by faith, not by sight . . .

2 Corinthians 5:7 (KJV)

Mt. Hood National Forest in Oregon

That's all I ask.
Walk. Just walk.
You don't have to run. Just
keep putting one foot . . .

In nothing be anxious, but in everything, by prayer and petition with thanksgiving, let your requests be made known to God. And the peace of God, which surpasses all understanding, will guard your hearts and your thoughts in Christ Jesus.

Philippians 4:6-7 (WEB)

Stone street in Spello, Italy

Stone stairway in Spello, Italy

in front
of the
other.

Even the youths shall faint and be weary, and the young men shall utterly fall: But they that wait upon the Lord shall renew *their* strength; they shall mount up with wings as eagles; they shall run, and not be weary; *and* they shall walk, and not faint.

Isaiah 40:30-31 (KJV)

41

Just keep going. Persevere to the end. Finish your course.

But as it is written, Eye hath not seen, nor ear heard, neither have entered into the heart of man, the things which God hath prepared for them that love him.

1 Corinthians 2:9 (KJV)

Mt. Hood National Forest in Oregon

Your faithful ancestors are watching and cheering for you from my kingdom. You cannot believe the rewards you will find on the other side of the finish line.

But you are a CHOSEN RACE, A royal PRIESTHOOD, A HOLY NATION, A PEOPLE FOR *GOD'S* OWN POSSESSION, so that you may proclaim the excellencies of Him who has called you out of darkness into His marvelous light . . .

1 Peter 2:9 (NASB)

Clouds over Lake Pontchartrain in New Orleans, Louisiana

There is nothing in this world to compare with the fruits of heaven.

"Bring the whole tithe into the storehouse, so that there may be food in My house, and test Me now in this," says the Lord of hosts, "if I will not open for you the windows of heaven and pour out for you a blessing until it overflows."

Malachi 3:10 (NASB)

Peristyle in City Park in New Orleans, Louisiana

Take all of the happiness you have ever known in this life . . .

~~~

Blessed *are* the merciful: for they shall obtain mercy.
Blessed *are* the pure in heart: for they shall see God.
Blessed *are* the peacemakers: for they shall be called the children of God.

Matthew 5:7-9 (KJV)

Yellow rose in Halifax, Canada

multiply it by quadrillion,
and you still would not come close
to the bliss—

In my Father's house are many mansions: if *it were* not so, I would have told you. I go to prepare a place for you.

John 14:2 (KJV)

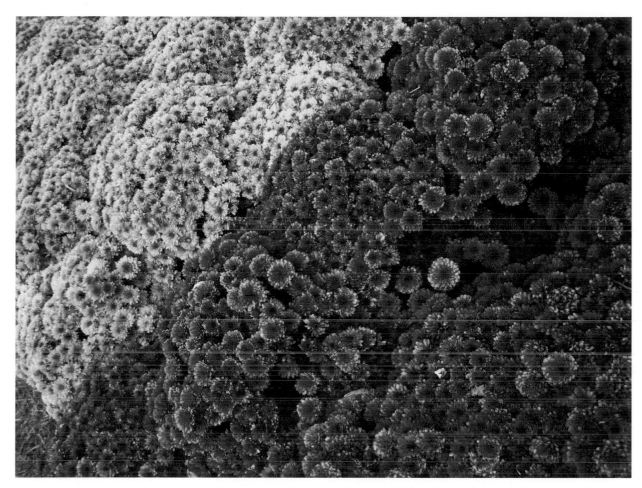

Biltmore gardens in Asheville, North Carolina

the absolute, perfect bliss—that awaits my good and faithful servants on the other side of the finish line.

For now we see through a glass, darkly; but then face to face: now I know in part; but then shall I know even as also I am known.

1 Corinthians 13:12 (KJV)

Bridge over a lagoon in City Park in New Orleans, Louisiana

Study to show yourself approved.
Feast on My Word.

I love those who love me;
Those who seek me diligently will find me.

Proverbs 8:17 (NASB)

*Child praying in the St. Jude shrine in Our Lady of Guadalupe
Church in New Orleans, Louisiana*

Learn of what I have done for those who
have preceded you on Earth,
and know that anything and everything I
have done for them, I will do for you.

Jabez called on the God of Israel, saying, "Oh that you would bless me indeed, and enlarge my border! May your hand be with me, and may you keep me from evil, that I may not cause pain!"

God granted him that which he requested.

1 Chronicles 4:10 (WEB)

Mt. Hood in Oregon

*You can have the prosperity and wisdom
of Solomon,
the strength and beauty of Esther,
the courage of David and Daniel.
Ask.*

Ask, and it will be given to you. Seek, and you will find. Knock, and it will be opened for you.

Matthew 7:7 (WEB)

Spanish moss in City Park in New Orleans, Louisiana

The doors of the storehouse are open.
Ask for what you require.
You have not because you ask not.
Trust me.

Come to Me, all who are weary and heavy-laden, and I will give you rest.

Matthew 11:28 (NASB)

Asheville, North Carolina

Turn all of your cares over to me.
You are my child.

Therefore humble yourselves under the mighty hand of God, that He may exalt you at the proper time, casting all your anxiety on Him, because He cares for you.

1 Peter 5:6-7 (NASB)

Mt. Hood National Forest in Oregon

*You are my good and faithful servant
in whom I am well pleased.
I made a covenant with your family
generations ago to bless you today.
I keep my promises.*

❡

Know therefore that the Lord your God, He is God,
the faithful God, who keeps His covenant and His
lovingkindness to a thousandth generation with those
who love Him and keep His commandments . . .

Deuteronomy 7:9 (NASB)

Cozumel, Mexico

Keep yours.
Give as I have given to you.
Love as I have loved you.

〉〈

A new commandment I give to you, that you love one another. Just as I have loved you, you also love one another. By this everyone will know that you are my disciples, if you have love for one another.

John 13:34-35 (WEB)

Couple sitting in City Park in New Orleans, Louisiana

Don't give in to Satan's message of doom and gloom. His days are numbered.

❥

Beloved, let us love one another, for love is of God; and everyone who loves has been born of God, and knows God. He who doesn't love doesn't know God, for God is love.

1 John 4:7-8 (WEB)

Oak trees in City Park in New Orleans, Louisiana

He is a toothless demon who has power if you give it to him by lending him the use of your mind.

⸻

Be of sober *spirit,* be on the alert. Your adversary, the devil, prowls around like a roaring lion, seeking someone to devour. But resist him, firm in *your* faith, knowing that the same experiences of suffering are being accomplished by your brethren who are in the world.

1 Peter 5:8-9 (NASB)

Oak trees in City Park in New Orleans, Louisiana

*Thoughts are powerful instruments
for good and evil.
On whose side are you today?
What are you thinking about?
Are you focusing on me or
the circumstances around you?*

Put on the full armor of God, so that you will be able to stand firm against the schemes of the devil.

Ephesians 6:11 (NASB)

Rainy day in Uptown New Orleans, Louisiana

Don't fall for Satan's smoke and mirrors.
You are safe and secure from all alarm.
Your fate is already sealed in blood.

I can do all things through Christ which strengtheneth me.

Philippians 4:13 (KJV)

La Sagrada Familia in Barcelona, Spain

Jesus died for your sins.

＜＞

. . . and, lo, I am with you always, *even* unto the end of the world. Amen.

Matthew 28:20 (KJV)

Lafayette Cemetery in New Orleans, Louisiana

Jesus prayed for you.

I do not ask You to take them out of the world, but to keep them from the evil *one*. They are not of the world, even as I am not of the world.

John 17:15-16 (NASB)

Sun peeking through clouds over Pozzuoli, Italy

You are mine.

Trust in the Lord with all your heart
And do not lean on your own understanding.
In all your ways acknowledge Him,
And He will make your paths straight.

Proverbs 3:5-6 (NASB)

Sunset over Lake Pontchartrain in New Orleans, Louisiana

*Focus on that fact and watch your life
come into focus.
Watch all those who were troubling you
bow before you.*

He will be like a tree planted by streams of water,
that produces its fruit in its season,
whose leaf also does not wither.
Whatever he does shall prosper.

Psalm 1:3 (WEB)

Trees next to water in City Park in New Orleans, Louisiana

Let my residence within you be seen by all.

You are the light of the world. A city set on a hill cannot be hidden; nor does *anyone* light a lamp and put it under a basket, but on the lampstand, and it gives light to all who are in the house. Let your light shine before men in such a way that they may see your good works, and glorify your Father who is in heaven.

Matthew 5:14-16 (NASB)

Positano, Italy, at night

Don't hide my light.
Share it.
Trust and obey.

⊱⟨⟩

"For I know the plans I have for you," declares the Lord, "plans for welfare and not for calamity, to give you a future and a hope."

Jeremiah 29:11 (NASB)

City Park in New Orleans, Louisiana

Afterword

The Lord bless you, and keep you;
The Lord make His face shine on you,
And be gracious to you;
The Lord lift up His countenance on you,
And give you peace.

Numbers 6:24-26 (NASB)

Sunset over Poplarville, Mississippi